THE Secret Message

For Arman and Leila
—M.J.

For Mum and Dad
—B.W.

Adapted and translated from "Parrot and the Merchant,"
from Book One of the Masnavi collection by Jalaledin Rumi, 13th century

Text copyright © 2010 by Mina Javaherbin
Illustrations copyright © 2010 by Bruce Whatley

First Edition · 10 9 8 7 6 5 4 3 2 1 · F850-6825-5-10196 · Printed in Singapore
Reinforced binding · Library of Congress Cataloging-in-Publication Data on file.
ISBN 978-1-4231-1044-6 · Visit www.hyperionbooksforchildren.com

THE
Secret
Message

— Based on a poem by Rumi —

WRITTEN BY **Mina Javaherbin**

ILLUSTRATED BY **Bruce Whatley**

Disney • HYPERION BOOKS
NEW YORK

MANY YEARS AGO, a wealthy Persian merchant kept a parrot from India in his shop at the bazaar. The bird, who once flew free in the Indian forests, now lived in a small cage.

Colorful tiles covered the shop's domed ceiling and walls, but the parrot preferred the beauty of the forest. All day the bird sang of longing. But the merchant would not let him go, because the parrot could sing and talk, and his bright feathers attracted customers to the shop. The parrot had helped the merchant become rich and famous.

One day, a group of wealthy traders walked by. Their sparkling cloaks reminded the parrot of the forest stars, and he called out to them. Enchanted by the bird, the traders entered the shop. Once inside, they purchased all the merchant's goods. The merchant rewarded the parrot with a large, golden cage.

That night at home, the merchant announced, "I'm going to India to buy more goods for my shop."

Everyone wanted something from India. The cook asked for extraordinary spices; the merchant's daughters asked for dazzling silk robes; and his wife requested brilliant jewels. The merchant promised to buy all the gifts.

Before he left on his trip, the merchant asked the parrot if he wanted anything from the place that had been his home. "An exotic flower or a silver cup, perhaps?"

"I don't want any gifts," the parrot said with a sigh. "But when you pass through the forest and see other parrots like me flying free, tell them I live far away. Tell them I miss flying with them, I miss their sweet voices, I miss the smell of the trees—"

The merchant interrupted, "But, Parrot, you live inside this wonderful golden cage with three swings."

"You're right," said the parrot. "Tell them about this cage."

"I will," said the merchant.

On the Silk Road, the caravan trudged over dry sand dunes, passed through steep green valleys, and braved dangerously narrow mountain paths. After a long journey, the travelers crossed the Indus River.

At the city of Gilgit, they saw temple dancers, monkeys, elephants, and cows enjoying a river festival. When they noticed the yogis who stayed calm in twisted poses, they knew they had arrived in India.

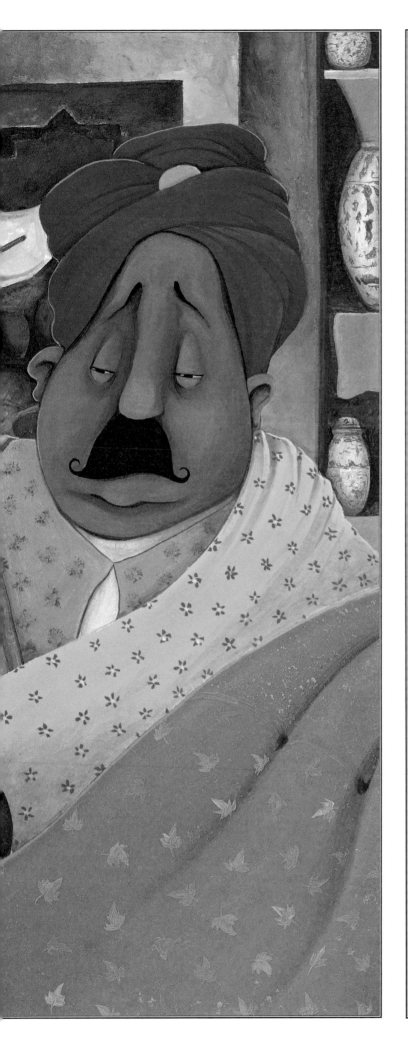

After the merchant made his purchases for the shop, he found brilliant jewels for his wife and sent men to the far corners of the market to buy rare spices for the cook. At the silk market, the merchant could not make up his mind—fabrics waved on display in a carnival of colors. Finally, the merchant picked a soft shade of pink with small red flowers and a bold blue fabric with a yellow leaf pattern for his daughters.

On the way back to Persia, the merchant's caravan passed through a thick tropical forest. He heard voices like his parrot's. He saw beautiful birds like his, flying free among the trees.

"Stop the caravan," ordered the merchant. He stepped down and asked the birds to gather around. "I have a message from your friend," he said. The parrots sat on twisted banyan tree branches and listened.

"Far away from India, I own a parrot that looks like you. He sent a message: he remembers flying in the forest, hearing your sweet voices, and smelling the trees. He lives inside a beautiful cage that I bought for him. It has three golden swings inside."

The birds listened carefully. Suddenly, one by one, they fell off the branches with their backs on the ground and their feet in the air. Their bodies lay still under the shadow of the banyan canopy.

The shocked merchant could not believe his eyes. The parrots stayed stiff on the ground. After a while, the merchant ordered his caravan to move on.

Once he was back in Persia, the merchant's family and friends celebrated his arrival with delicious food prepared by the cook, using his new Indian spices. Dancers paraded in the courtyard to tambourines and harp as the merchant told tall tales about his journey. He left out the part about the parrots in the forest.

At his shop, the merchant busied himself with storing the new goods. He avoided the parrot.

One quiet afternoon the parrot asked, "Merchant, when you were in India, did you deliver my message?"

"Parrot, something bad happened in the forest. I don't wish to talk about it."

"For years I have sung for you in a cage," said the parrot. "I didn't ask for jewels or spices. I only asked you to deliver a message for me. Is this how you repay me?"

"Well, if you insist, I will tell you. I did indeed deliver your message to the birds. They listened, and then, suddenly, they all fell off the tree branches, not one breathing a single breath."

The parrot listened. Then, as soon as the merchant stopped talking, he fell off his golden swing with his feet pointing up to the sky. Not a single breath came out of him.

The merchant ran to the cage. "What have I done?" he cried. "Have I caused your death?"

The parrot stayed still at the bottom of the cage. The merchant knew that this parrot would never bring another customer to his shop.

He took the stiff bird out of the cage and placed him on the counting table.

In an instant, the parrot fluttered his wings and soared up to the shop's domed ceiling.

"You're alive!" the merchant said.

"More alive than ever, Merchant, thanks to the message from my friends in India!"

Then the parrot flew away through the hole in the domed ceiling, and all the way to India, to fly free among his friends.

Author's Note

WHEN I WAS A CHILD, growing up in Iran, I begged my father every evening to tell me the story of the parrot and the merchant. It was a tale he told from memory. I still remember the fantastic scenes that played in my imagination as he spoke.

Years later, when I studied Persian literature, I discovered my favorite bedtime story was actually an ancient poem. The poet was Rumi, the famous literary figure who lived in Persia hundreds of years ago, in the 13th century.

Discovering this familiar story from my childhood in an important work of literature was the start of a lifelong passion for books. Today, I continue to crack open big, dusty volumes in search of small treasures . . . and secret messages.